Verona

Stefano Zuffi

Verona

Electa

Introduction
The first part of the guide is a brief survey of the historical events and urbanistic transformations that have shaped the city.

The Visit
The second part of the guide outlines a series of itineraries. This section opens with a *general plan* of the city which indicates the churches, palaces and other points of interest, each of which is later treated with a descriptive text.
The *sites* and *monuments* described appear in bold-face type.
Titles of *works of art* are printed in italics.
Each itinerary is introduced by a text that highlights the most important sites and monuments.
Sites and *monuments* are followed by grid coordinates which refer to the structure of the map. They are listed in logical sequence, in keeping with the course of a given itinerary, and each is accompanied by an account of its history, artistic significance, modifications, and present state.

Supplements
A *selected bibliography*, organized chronologically, allows the reader to further investigate the themes addressed in this volume. The alphabetical *index of sites* at the end of the guide provides quick reference to the various sites and monuments described in the itineraries.

Translation
Jeffrey Jennings

On the cover
Bernardo Bellotto, *Ideal View of Verona*, Philadelphia Museum of Art.

© 1995 by **Electa**, Milan
Elemond Editori Associati

Contents

History and Urban Development

The fascination of Verona's urbanistic, architectural and artistic character is the result of a long historical evolution coupled with the distinctiveness of its geographical location. The modern city, an economic center of great importance and a major hub of commercial traffic between northern Italy and Europe, is seamlessly coextensive with the city's ancient core. Verona has been able to conserve its artistic heritage practically intact, and continues to offer a unique urban atmosphere characterized by a compact network of streets, dense with magnificent buildings from various epochs.

In the interest of clarity, the guide has been organized into four different itineraries. Such a subdivision, dictated by reasons of practicality and by the disposition of the monuments, was not easy to decide upon: indeed, it doesn't take long for the visitor to discover that the most telling aspect of this magnificent city lies in the strict coherence that links together the various quarters of the historic center. The city as a whole, ensconced within the ample walls that protect the banks of the river, is like a dense monumental palimpsest, with a continuous and well-distributed array of Roman ruins, medieval churches, memories of the della Scala reign, elegant palaces, Renaissance additions, and testimony of the city's former role as a military stronghold. Weaving among Verona's imposing edifices, solemn custodians of history which dominate the city, is a tight network of streets and squares of great evocative power—some of these are famous and thus often crowded with tourists, while others remain relatively secret, hidden among the folds of the city. The river Adige, whose banks serve as an endless balcony from which to enjoy stupendous views, is a fundamental "presence," the city's principal point of reference—indeed, it is from the Adige that one can take in virtually the entire history of Verona at a glance.

A quick look at the map of the city and one realizes the particularity of the situation created by the river: on the right, a sharp bend delineates and protects a narrow promontory across which extends the tightly ordered checkerboard of

Opposite page
Stefano da Zevio, Madonna of the Rose Garden, detail. Museo di Castelvecchio.

Caspar van Wittel, View of the Adige at Verona. Florence, Galleria Palatina.

The Arena

streets and squares; just beyond the embankments on the left, by contrast, rise the foothills of the Lessi mountains, functioning as a sort of natural fortification. The riverbed itself is wide, but prior to the building up of the banks that was completed during the last century, it had never been difficult to cross. This favorable geographical circumstance was certainly exploited in ancient times, but it has been as yet impossible to ascertain the identity of the first permanent population, nor do we know the origins of the city's name, though it remains unchanged over time. These first inhabitants (perhaps Euganians or Rhaetians) were succeeded by the Etruscans and the Celtic line of the Cenomanian Gauls. At the beginning of the 1st century B.C. the city became a Roman colony, lying close to the border of Republican Rome's Italian territories. With the rapid expansion of the Empire toward the Alps, Verona assumed a key role in the roadway system, and became an important center of commerce and transportation. Three consular roads converged there (the Gallica, Claudia Augusta and Postumia), and its circle of walls made it exceptionally secure. The city itself was concentrated at the bend in the river, while the left bank, also protected by walls and fortifications, hosted the theater and the acropolis. The river was spanned by two bridges, one of which (the Ponte Pietra) is still in use today. The exemplary organization of Verona during the Roman era is for the most part still in evidence, thanks not only to numerous surviving structures but also because the urban layout established around the 1st century A.D. has been the guide for all subsequent developments, and thus has not undergone profound change: Piazza delle Erbe, for example, is simply a medieval modification of the ancient forum, where the straight boulevards running from the Porta Borsari and the Porta dei Leoni intersect.

Surely the most spectacular vestiges of Roman times are the monuments, so grandiose and well-preserved as to make Verona one of the principal archeological centers in Italy. The most outstanding is the Arena, used today for the staging of extravagant opera productions, but no less significant are the ruins of the theater, set into the steep slope of the hill on the other side of the Adige, and the two Roman entry gates mentioned above. Excavated materials are housed in the Museo Archeologico, a suggestive reworking of the remains of the theater, and in the Maffei collection of epigraphy.

The Scaligere Tombs, Sarcophagus of Cangrande I della Scala. Santa Maria Antica.

In the second half of the 3rd century the emperor Gallienus had the city walls expanded to encompass the Arena, a measure of the threat of barbarian invasions and of the ever-increasing pressures on territorial borders.

The fall of the Roman Empire was followed by the long sprawl of the Middle Ages, which would not come to a close until the 12th century. Under the rule of the Ostrogoths, the Longobards, the Franks and the German emperors, Verona nevertheless remained a lively, wealthy and cultured city. By the 4th century the "Christianization" of Verona was brought to completion by St. Zeno, the city's first bishop and patron saint. Theodoric built a palace here, using it in alternation with his residence in Ravenna; Albion, Pepin and Berengarius also chose the strategic city on the Adige as their head-

St. Zeno the Fisherman and the Messengers of Gallienus, bronze door panel. San Zeno.

The Scaligere Tombs, Equestrian statue of Mastino II della Scala, detail of the tomb of Mastino II.

quarters. Only a few traces of early medieval architecture survive, mostly in the form of small churches and humble votive chapels; the Paleochristian basilicas were largely renovated during the Romanesque period. The 9th and 10th centuries witnessed the birth of the cathedral's *scriptorium*, thus inaugurating a tradition of illuminated manuscripts that would reach its highest expression in the Renaissance.

The cultural initiatives promoted by the archdeacon Pacifico and the king Berengarius were violently interrupted by the disastrous sack of the city at the hands of the Hungarians in the 10th century. As part of the region of Bavaria, Verona was for a time a southern outpost of the Holy Roman Empire. The historical connection with Germany (today, Verona links the Brenner Pass with the Po valley) has always been strong, even after the city had gained its independence.

From 1107 Verona enjoyed almost three centuries of autonomy and power, first as a proud and free city-state and later under the rule of the prosperous della Scala family. The stylistic categories that correspond to these two periods, the Romanesque and the Gothic, manifest themselves in Verona at their highest and most original, in architecture, sculpture and paintings of extraordinary importance. During the the 12th century Verona formed, along with Vicenza, Padua and Treviso, the Verona League; after having resisted Barbarossa's attempted siege in 1164, the Veronese aligned themselves with the Lombard League in the epic Battle of Legnano. Construction activity during this period was intense, as witnessed by churches such as Santa Trinita, San Lorenzo and

The Bra gates and the pentagonal Cittadella tower, erected by Gian Galeazzo Visconti.

Pisanello, St. George and the Princess. Sant'Anastasia, sacristy.

Santo Stefano, and by numerous civic buildings—not to mention the luminous volumes of two major masterpieces of Romanesque architecture: the Duomo, and above all the marvelous basilica of San Zeno, originally a Benedictine abbey church. Both sites dedicate significant space to decorative sculptural programs, executed by Masters Nicolò and Guglielmo and other craftsmen whose names do not survive. Important examples of medieval wall painting, which until the 13th century maintained a largely Byzantine character, can be found in San Zeno, San Fermo and the Museo degli Affreschi housed at Juliet's Tomb. In the course of the 13th century the city was fraught with internal power struggles, vicious enough to have elicited an admonishment from Dante—the story of Romeo and Juliet rendered tragic by the bloody feud between the Capuleti and Montecchi families, is so familiar as to have become proverbial. Indeed, the omnipresence of the two heroes of Luigi da Porto's novella and Shakespeare's more famous tragedy in the souvenir booths has become quite tiresome, and there is no lack of medieval sites that falsely claim to be the houses and tombs of the unfortunate lovers. In 1227, the blood-thirsty Ezzelino da Romano rose to power, his tyrannic rule lasting for more than thirty years, until 1259. In 1260, Mastino I, head of the noble della Scala family, was elected podesta and captain of the people, and his descendants continued to govern until the end of the next century. The della Scala dynasty, among the more refined courts of Gothic Europe, found its greatest exemplar in Cangrande I. Ruler of Verona from 1308 to 1329, Cangrande pledged his fidelity to the emperor rather than the Church, he augmented Veronese possessions, and further distinguished himself through a far-

Michele Sanmicheli,
the Porta Palio

sighted cultural patronage, exemplified by the hospitality offered to Dante, who dedicated his *Paradiso* to Cangrande.

The della Scala era coincides with the most characteristic and fruitful period of Veronese art. The exuberant and fantastical forms of the Gothic give life to architectural and sculptural gems such as the churches of Sant'Anastasia and San Fermo Maggiore, and the renowned Scaligere Tombs, grand funereal monuments to the della Scala rulers in the form of highly ornamented baldachins; other important examples of Veronese sculpture are displayed in the Museo di Castelvecchio. Giotto's passage through Verona and the activities of local masters such as Turone and Altichiero form the basis of the native pictorial tradition, solid and distinctive enough to have sustained and developed the themes and modes of the courtly Gothic style even after the fall of the della Scala.

The concern with defending the city and demonstrating its power, pursued throughout the 14th century, manifests itself in a series of military construction projects: the Castelvecchio, the Ponte Scaligero, and a new and more heavily fortified circle of ramparts. On October 18, 1387, however, Antonio della Scala was forced to flee the invasion staged by Gian Galeazzo Visconti, duke of Milan. Verona lost its independence, and for about twenty years its rulership was contested by the Visconti (who held the city until 1404), the Carraresi, and finally the Venetian Republic. Venice's reign began on June 23, 1405, was confirmed by the Golden Bull on July 16, 1406, lasted for the next four centuries, with a brief interruption between 1509 and 1517, during which time Verona was a fiefdom of the Hapsburg emperor, Maximillian.

The long reign of the Venetian Republic ensured to Verona a peaceful prosperity, clearly evidenced by its artistic activity. During the first half of the 15th century, Verona was one of the capitals of the International Gothic style, integrating the rationalist discoveries of the Paduan renaissance with the extraordinary refinement of the works of Pisanello and Stefano da Zevio. The magnificent triptych painted by Mantegna for San Zeno (1459) signals the beginning of a new phase. While certain churches kept in step with the transition from the Gothic to the Renaissance (San Bernardino, Santa Maria in Organo, the interior of the Duomo), the Verona school of painting was essentially a group of masters specializing in the decoration of altars and family chapels. Humanists and bibliophiles stimulated and sustained instead the activities of the manuscript illuminators, with the aim of establishing Verona as a center of book production—a tradition that continues today with the presence of major publishing houses. A separate chapter in the the history of late-15th-century Veronese art is reserved for the astonishing *intarsia* work executed by Fra Giovanni da Verona for Santa Maria in Organo. Fra Giocondo's Loggia marks the beginning of the mature phase of the Renaissance in Verona. The 16th century opens with a reawakened awareness of the city's historical identity: its Roman origins are investigated, it competes with other cities for the honor of calling itself home to famous Latin poets, its ancient monuments are reconsidered and used as models for churches, public buildings and palaces. Fundamental was the work of Michele Sanmicheli, the renowned military engineer who also gave to Verona many refined works of civic and reli-

Paolo Veronese, Madonna Enthroned with Saints and Donors (Bevilacqua-Lazise Altarpiece), detail. Museo di Castelvecchio.

gious architecture: the renovation of the ramparts and city gates, the bell tower of the Duomo, the splendid Bevilacqua and Pompei palaces, the cupola of San Giorgio in Braida, the facade of Santa Maria in Organo and numerous other projects. Few cities can boast a richness of Renaissance painting on a par with that of Verona. In keeping with medieval practice, entire families of artists passed the painter's trade from father to son: typical are the Badile, Caroto, Morone and dai Libri families. The list of important Veronese masters of the 15th and 16th centuries is long: to name but a few, Nicolò Giolfino, Liberale da Verona, Paolo Morando, Francesco Bonsignori and Bonifacio de Pitati. Unfortunately, many of the painted facades of private Renaissance palaces have been erased by the passage of time thus leaving us without a true sense of the precious mosaic of exterior wall painting that had once earned Verona fame as *urbis picta*, or "painted city." The works of the local school of painting can be found in many churches, and is well represented in the collections of the Museo di Castelvecchio. The most talented local artists, however, were drawn away to Venice, as was the case with the great Paolo Caliari, known as Veronese. He left his native city while still young and only returned occasionally, for just long enough to leave precious traces of his inimitable style, the epitome of enthusiasm for color, light and classical beauty.

Verona then began to decline in importance, its fame during the 17th and 18th centuries linked above all to its scholars and intellectuals. One should not, however, underestimate the achievements of the painters of the 17th century, in part reminiscent of the splendors of Paolo Veronese, but at the same time open to the innovations of Caravaggio. The pursuits of the Humanists presently take the form of the Museo Maffeiano, public libraries and cultural organizations, and the garden of the Palazzo Giusti, once the site of outdoor literary *salons*. The scientific and cultural heritage of the city lives on in the university, in the theaters and in a rich array of museums, among which is excellent natural history collection.

The peaceful period of Venetian rule was abruptly interrupted in 1796 by the tumultuous arrival of Napoleon's army and the fall of the Republic of Venice, casting Verona into a vortex of international tensions. After centuries of tranquillity, the strategic position of the city as the key to military control of the Brenner Pass and the eastern part of the Po Valley proved to be the cause of its downfall. Ceded to Austria by the Treaty of Campoformio (1797), in 1801 it came to be divided literally in half: the French took the right bank of the Adige, and the Austrians took the left, less extensive but equipped with important military facilities. A famous episode from Napoleonic era is the popular insurrection known as the "Pasque Veronesi," brutally and bloodily suppressed. In 1805 the city was placed under the French protectorate and became part of the Kingdom of Italy; with the fall of Napoleon, it went back to the Austrian Empire. The great fortifications of the della Scala epoch (such as Castel San Pietro) were transformed into block-houses, barracks, casemates and powder magazines. Verona, by now reduced to an immense military outpost, be-

Sant'Anastasia, apse and bell tower.

Michele Sanmicheli, Porta Nuova (reworked in the 19th century).

Opposite page
View from the left bank of the Adige: the Ponte Pietra, and the apse and bell tower of the Duomo.

The banks of the Adige photographed in 1866 by Moritz Lotze, prior to the disastrous floods which led to the construction of high stone embankments.

came the crucial point of the quadrilateral defensive network whose other three points were Mantua, Peschiera and Legnago. Many of the key events of the Risorgimento and the war of independence unfolded at Verona and on its outlying battlefields. Finally, on October 16, 1866, a few months after the second battle of Custoza, Verona was liberated.

In 1882 a devastating flood of the Adige forced the construction of new and higher embankments. The city's relationship with the river was thus radically changed, signaling the birth of modern Verona and the continuous growth of its economic importance and population. Heavily bombarded in both world wars, Verona has had to learn to bounce back, to present itself as a city with two faces. On the one hand, it has meticulously and lovingly preserved its historical and artistic patrimony, without ever altering its intimate character and atmosphere. The Arena's opera season, the classical and Shakespearean productions at the Roman theater, and the major exhibitions of contemporary art at the Palazzo Forti attract a constant flow of visitors to the city. On the other hand, Verona forcefully asserts itself as a modern center of encounter and exchange. The monuments damaged or destroyed by the wars have been restored with great care: to rebuild demolished bridges, the Veronese fished the original stones from the Adige, while the restoration and installation of the Castelvecchio by Carlo Scarpa represents a milestone in Italian museum design. Verona's role as a crossroads of highway and rail traffic makes it one of today's principal markets of the exchange of agricultural products, chemicals and pharmaceuticals between Italy and Europe. Its trade fair enjoys global prestige. The proximity of the Lago di Garda helps make Verona a major point of reference for international culture and vacationing, underscored yet further by its stimulating mix of contemporaneity, art and history.

Francesco Bonsignori, Madonna and Child. Museo di Castelvecchio.

These twin aspects of the city's soul coexist without conflict: every time one returns to Verona one reexperiences the pleasure and emotion of being in a city whose serene and confident participation in the present is firmly rooted in a luminous past, reflected in its equilibrated urban disposition and a pervasive atmosphere of good taste. In sum, it is a harmony that perfectly integrates the oval of the Roman amphitheater with the Gothic towers of the della Scala epoch, medical and technological innovation with Romanesque basilicas, modern vivacity with ancient majesty, creating a unique flavor that conquers the heart of every visitor. Dante was among those who recognized this, finding in the hospitality "the first refuge" of his exile, as was Shakespeare, according to whom "there is no other world beyond the walls of Verona."

Following page
*Map of the historic center
of Verona.*

*The Brenzoni monument,
sculpture by Nanni di
Bartolo, fresco by Pisanello.
San Fermo Maggiore.*

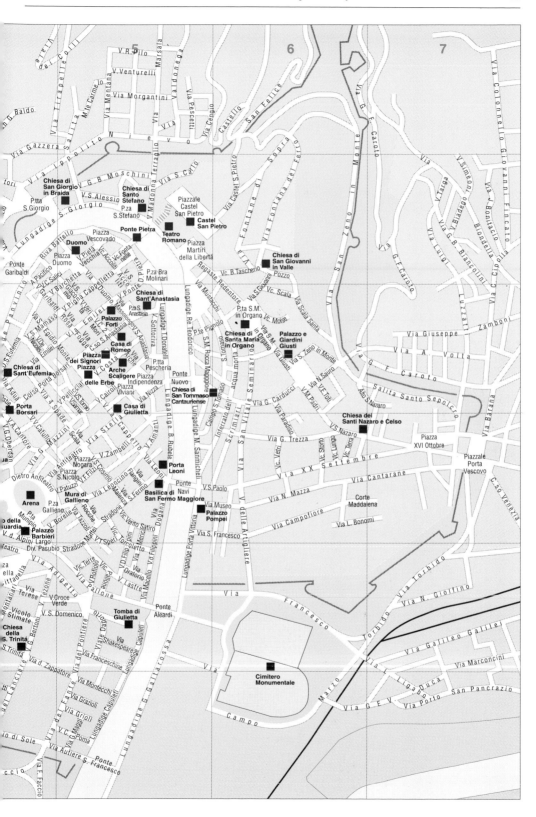

The Medieval Heart of Verona: From Piazza delle Erbe to the Adige

This is an itinerary dense with monuments from various epochs, unravelling entirely within the limits of the Roman city in a tangle of highly evocative streets, squares and urban ambients. It should be undertaken on foot, at a leisurely pace so as to allow frequent stops and digressions, not only to admire the more famous edifices but also to appreciate the web of ancient houses, palaces and ruins that so strongly characterize the historic center of Verona. This area corresponds to the tip of the "promontory" defined by the curve of the Adige.

Our point of departure is the Roman **Porta Borsari**, which gives its name to the elegant boulevard that follows the ancient course of the city's principle east-west axis. After having stopped by the churches of **Sant'Eufemia** (on Via Emilei) and **San Giovanni in Foro**, one reaches the unforgettable **Piazza delle Erbe**. The dramatically longitudinal space occupies the site of the Roman forum and is entirely surrounded by monumental buildings, a stylistic parade that links Romanesque, Gothic, Renaissance and Baroque.

We then head toward Via Cappello, along which lie the remains of the roadbed of the main Roman north-south axis. On the left, the customary stop at the **House of Juliet**. The street terminates at the ruins of the **Porta dei Leoni**, not far from the Adige and the basilica of San Fermo.

Returning back toward Piazza delle Erbe, a brief detour down Via Stella takes us past the church of **Santa Maria della Scala** and other points of interest; to reach the Piazza, one follows the last stretch of the lively Via Mazzini.

This most well-trodden of Verona's tourist routes resumes, beyond the **Arco della Costa**, with the complex formed by the **Palazzo della Ragione** and other buildings looking out upon the **Piazza dei Signori**. A few more steps and one comes upon the bizarre spectacle of the **Scaligere Tombs**, a gloriously mad Gothic fantasy.

Creating an entirely different atmosphere is Via Sottoriva, a series of ancient porticoes that leads to the apse end of the great Dominican church of **Sant'Anastasia**, a treasury of illustrious works of art, most notable of which is Pisanello's fresco depicting *St. George and the Princess*.

The final destination on our itinerary is the **Duomo**, or cathedral, just two hundred meters from Sant'Anastasia by way of Via Massalongo (where one finds the **Palazzo Forti**) and Via Duomo, though you might prefer any of the many fascinating alternative routes. For those who wish to penetrate the heart of the aristocratic quarter, proceed along Via Emilei, Via Garibaldi (address of the **Palazzo Miniscalchi-Erizzo**, which hosts a small, elegant museum) and the avenue of Arcidiacono Pacifico, thereby arriving before the cathedral's facade. Otherwise, you might pass behind the splendid apse of Sant'Anastasia and, walking along the river in the direction of the **Ponte Pietra**, you'll arrive at a cluster of scenic squares that announce the apse of the Duomo. It would be prudent to allow ample time for your visit to the complex of monuments encompassed by the cathedral: the **Baptistry**, the little church of **Sant'Elena**, and the **Vescovado**, which looks out upon a quiet and charming piazza.

Opposite page
Pisanello, St. George and the Princess, detail. Sant'Anastasia, sacristy.

The towers and churches of the historic center, embraced by the bend of the Adige.

Porta Borsari.

Sant'Eufemia, facade.

PORTA BORSARI AND CORSO DI PORTA BORSARI (C4). Fascinating backdrop of a long and elegant boulevard, **Porta Borsari** was built in the 1st century as a monumental entrance to the city at the western end of the main east-west axis; outside the gate is a "holy road," which includes the Arco dei Gavi. Set tightly between buildings from a later period, the Porta can be read as a symbol of the living presence of Roman ruins in the heart of Verona. The name refers to the *bursarii*, medieval functionaries who collected tithes and tolls for the bishop. The exterior facade is practically intact: disposed above the two supporting arches is a double course of arched windows. The tympana and architraves that articulate the spaces were admired in the Renaissance as being an ideal lexicon of classical motifs, and as such were borrowed by Sanmicheli in his designs for the facades of aristocratic palaces.

The **Corso di Porta Borsari** runs from the Porta to Piazza delle Erbe. It is characterized by occasional Roman ruins, ancient homes and palaces, and on the left, the lovely flank of the small Romanesque church of **San Giovanni in Foro**.

Parallel to the Corso is the elegant Via Emilei, from which rises the Gothic brick church of **Sant'Eufemia**, founded by the Augustinian friars at the end of the 13th century. Its narrow and elongated plan is most distinctive: the long flank overlooks Via Emilei, while the monolithic facade, relieved by two-mullioned windows and a 15th-century portal, opens out onto a small piazza. Numerous paintings from the 16th to 18th centuries are conserved in its totally modified interior.

PIAZZA DELLE ERBE (C5). Epicenter of the city's ancient core, Verona's own living stage-set continues to maintain its historical function as a marketplace. It's long and narrow form follows that of the Roman forum that once occupied this same site. The central zone, called the "toloneo," is thick with the broad white umbrellas of the market stands. The cobblestones (roughly a meter square) are still used as a unit of mea-

*Piazza delle Erbe.
In the foreground, the
column with the Lion
of St. Mark.*

sure for determining the rental price of sales space. Between
the market stands are various columns and monuments: com-
ing from Corso di Porta Borsari one encounters, in order, the
column of the **Lion of St. Mark** (1523); the beautiful **Fontana
di Madonna Verona** (1386), a reworking of a Roman statue
probably erected by Bonino da Campione for Cansignorio della Scala; the 16th-century **berlina**, an aedicula used to cele-
brate the inauguration of rulers; and the **market column**
(1401), resting atop an aedicula, built by Gian Galeazzo Visconti to display the emblems of the duchy of Milan, which
owes its name to the official commercial standards of measure
inscribed on the stairs and pilasters.

The entire periphery of the piazza is framed by an uninterrupted series of ancient buildings, alternating between
simple houses and austere monumental complexes of various
epochs. At one end stands the crenellated 14th-century **Torre
del Gardello**, with the city's oldest bells; its sloped roof was
added in 1626. Next to it is the exuberant facade of the **Palazzo Maffei** (1668), with its statues of pagan deities and balus-
trades, one of the finest examples of Baroque architecture in
Verona. On the right side of the piazza, on the corner of Via
Pellicciai, is the **Casa dei Mercanti**, a reconstruction of the
late-Romanesque building of 1301. Across from it are the 16th-
century **Case Mazzanti**, a group of houses joined by a portico
and decorated with festive mythological frescoes, followed by
the **Arco della Costa**, or "Arch of the Rib" (so named for the
whale bones that hang from the vault), which opens onto the
adjacent Piazza dei Signori. Next, the neoclassical facade of
the **Palazzo del Comune** by Giuseppe Barbieri. Soaring
above it all is the **Torre dei Lamberti**, a slender shaft of brick
fully eight-four meters tall, erected by the Lamberti family at
the end of the 12th century and completed in the mid-15th century with a beautiful octagonal crown. The tower is accessible
to visitors from the courtyard of the Palazzo del Comune, offering spectacular views of the city.

*Piazza delle Erbe, Palazzo
del Comune and the Torre
dei Lamberti.*

House of Juliet

Porta dei Leoni

VIA CAPPELLO (D5). Coextensive with the main Roman north-south axis, Via Cappello still bears traces of the ancient roadbed, as well as the base of a defense tower at the Porta Leoni. Leaving Piazza delle Erbe, one encounters almost immediately on the left the so-called **House of Juliet**, ubiquitous tourist magnet of questionable authenticity and taste. The fiction is rendered credible by the modifications made to a genuine 13th-century "palazzetto," including the addition of a little balcony. The street ends at the scenic ruins of the **Porta dei Leoni** (1st century A.D.), one of the most refined and unusual archeological sites in Verona. Attached to a residential building, approximately half of it remains: the one surviving arch is crowned by a tympanum, above which runs a series of framed arch windows and, yet further up, a fragment of an exedra measured out by fluted columns. Nearby are the rich collections of the **Biblioteca Civica**, or public library.

Giovanni Badile, The Life of St. Jerome, detail. Santa Maria della Scala, Guantieri Chapel.

To return to Piazza delle Erbe and resume our tour of the surrounding area, a brief detour down Via Stella, Via Scala and Via Mazzini is advised. Animated by pedestrian traffic and local trade, these streets are lined with numerous monumental edifices, some of which were unfortunately damaged by bombing. Such is the case of the so-called **Palazzo dei Diamanti** (1582), which derives its name from the rusticated facade, reconstructed after the Second World War, similar to that of the famous Ferrarese palace of the same name. Serious damage was also suffered by the church of **Santa Maria della Scala**, a 14th-century structure built by Cangrande I, though ample traces of the original Gothic exterior survive intact. The interior, however, has been almost entirely renovated except for a few works of art, among which is an important fresco cycle by Giovanni Badile (1443–44). Not far from here is the church of **San Nicolò**, built in 1627 by Lelio Pellesina, perhaps the highest expression of Baroque religious architecture in Verona. Though its facade, reassembled from the demolished church of San Sebastiano and applied after the war, is neoclassical, the interior preserves the original Baroque richness of form, with statuary and paintings from the 17th century.

PIAZZA DEI SIGNORI (C5). From the animation of Piazza delle Erbe one passes with a certain abruptness into the severe elegance of Piazza dei Signori, surrounded in part by porticoes and enclosed entirely by arcades, almost like an interior courtyard. It is populated by numerous statues, disposed along the arches, the portals and the copings of the buildings. Political and administrative center of Verona under both the della Scala and the Venetian Republic, the piazza is graced at its center by the 19th-century **Dante Memorial**, tribute to the poet's stay in the overlooking palazzo of the della Scala family. To the right is the side of the **Palazzo del Comune**, or city hall: the Romanesque structure of the building (1193) is easily discernable beneath the modifications made during the Renaissance. Inside is the well-preserved and elegant **Old Market Courtyard**, a pilastered portico opened by beautiful Romanesque triple-mullioned windows which stand

out against a surface decorated with alternating bands of red and white. On the right springs forth the buoyant exterior staircase, jewel of the late-Gothic (15th century).

On this same side is the **Palazzo dei Tribunali**, a composite of various epochs: particularly striking are the massive della Scala tower, the 16th-century interventions of Sanmicheli and, in the early Renaissance courtyard, the Porta dei Bombardieri, paragon of 17th-century taste. At the rear of the piazza is the **Palazzo del Governo**, former residence of the della Scala, cradle of 14th-century Veronese culture. The present building is in large part a reconstruction from the 1930s, though significant portions of the original structure remain in the porticoed courtyard and the loggia.

The left side of Piazza dei Signori is occupied by its most important building, the **Loggia di Fra Giocondo**, so named for its presumed architect. Built between 1476 and 1493, the Loggia signals a definitive break from the Gothic in favor of a refined interpretation of the Renaissance distinguished by the harmony of proportions, the considered elegance of materials and color, and the abundant sculptural decoration. Above the eight arches of the graceful portico is a *piano nobile* with ample double-mullioned windows alternating with broad pilaster strips; along the cornice are five statues of illustrious citizens of the Roman era, the city's homage to its own Latin origins.

Piazza dei Signori, Loggia di Fra Giocondo.

Opposite page
Piazza dei Signori with the Dante Memorial. In the background, the Palazzo del Governo.

Piazza dei Signori, the tower of the Palazzo dei Tribunali and the Palazzo del Comune.

Piazza dei Signori, Palazzo dei Tribunali.

Piazzetta delle Arche Scaligere, Tomb of Cansignorio. Behind, Santa Maria Antica.

THE SCALIGERE TOMBS (C5). From the arcade between the Palazzo del Governo and the Palazzo dei Tribunali one enters a small piazza, transformed in the 14th century into an extravagant triumph of Gothic fantasy. Within a splendid enclosure of flexible iron mesh bearing the della Scala coat of arms are gathered the grandiose funerary arks of the lords of Verona. The family cemetery is comprised of various sarcophagi and, rather more spectacularly, three enormous tombs covered by baldachins, which are in turn capped with pointed spires bearing equestrian portraits of the deceased and surrounded by a multitude of statues and decorative sculpture. Aside from the quality of the individual details fashioned by master stonemasons from Lombardy, Tuscany and the Veneto, the most striking aspect is the sumptuous and extravagant effect of the whole. The three major tombs belong to *Mastino II*, begun in 1345 (prior to his death), characterized by trilobate arches; *Cansignorio* (1375), a work by Bonino da Campione, rich to the point of excess in pinnacles, statuary, tabernacles and aediculae; and *Cangrande I* (d. 1329), suspended over the portal of Santa Maria Antica. Built by the so-called Master of the Architrave of Sant'Anastasia, the Tomb of Cangrande is the indisputable masterpiece of Veronese sculpture in the age of the della Scala. The equestrian statue seen here is a copy of the original, which is conserved at the Museo di Castelvecchio.

The tiny church of **Santa Maria Antica**, which harks back to the Longobard era, is now characterized by the nobly austere Romanesque forms of its reconstruction in 1185, most notably the conical spire and solemn interior.

From the Scaligere Tombs we can head toward Sant'Anastasia, passing by the alleged **House of Romeo**, a small 14th-century brick building with a crenellated cornice. Crossing Piazza Independenza and Via Pescheria Vecchia, we come upon the evocative **Via Sottoriva**, a typical residential street along the Adige, lined with ancient porticoed houses.

Piazza Sant'Anastasia

SANT'ANASTASIA (C5). The largest church in Verona, it was built by the Dominicans in the Gothic style, starting in 1290 and completed in the 15th century. The imposing facade, only the lower part of which is fully finished, is centered upon the fabulous twin *portal* from the early 14th century, with the Life of Christ and other images carved into the architrave. To the left of the facade is a picturesque group of 14th-century brick and stone structures (the entrance to the convent, surmounted by the *Tomb of Guglielmo Castelbarco* beneath a baldachin fixed to an exterior wall of the small church of **San Giorgietto**, the interior of which is decorated with Gothic frescoes).

For an excellent view of Sant'Anastasia's bell tower, one must continue around the exterior the church toward its slender Gothic apse overlooking the Adige.

The interior is characterized by a simple yet imposing system of pointed arches, enriched by exuberant late-Gothic and Renaissance decoration. Altars, frescoes and reliefs constitute a veritable anthology of Veronese art from the 14th through the 16th centuries. The floor, designed by Pietro da Porlezza in 1462, is original. The first two pilasters of the central nave bear the popular 16th-century *holy water fonts*, seemingly supported by the so-called "gobbi," or hunchback statues. The aisles offer a parade of grand chapels, decorated with altarpieces and frescoes by Veronese painters of the 15th and

Sant'Anastasia, twin portal with the Life of Christ on the architrave.

Tomb of Guglielmo di Castelbarco.

Altichiero, The Cavalli Family Before the Virgin. Sant'Anastasia, Cavalli Chapel.

Holy water font, with the statue known as "the hunchback." Sant'Anastasia, central nave.

16th centuries (Liberale da Verona, Nicolò Giolfino, Francesco Morone, Francesco Caroto). At the beginning of the right aisle is the great *Fregoso Altarpiece* (c. 1560) by Sanmicheli, with sculptural decorations by Danese Cattaneo. Equally noteworthy is the *St. Thomas of Aquinus Altar*, built in the late 15th century in the right transept, decorated with an altarpiece by Gerolamo dai Libri. The architectural and decorative complex of *apsidal chapels*, once individually owned by noble families, is of great importance as well. The last on the right hosts the tombs of the Cavalli family and a number of 14th-century frescoes, among which is the votive scene of *The Cavalli Family Before the Virgin*, painted in the 1390s by Altichiero, the most important work remaining in the city of this expressive Veronese Gothic painter, for the most part active in Padua. Next to it is the *Pellegrini Chapel*, decorated by Michele da Firenze (c. 1435) with terra cotta panels in high relief. In the presbytery, against a background of a 14th-century fresco of *The Last Judgement*, is the *Serego Tomb* (c. 1425), typical example of Veronese funereal art of that time, attributed to the sculptor Nanni di Bartolo and the painter Michele Giambono. Both apsidal chapels on the left are decorated with 14th-century frescoes.

From the left transept (graced by a notable altarpiece by Francesco Morone), we can pass into the lovely 15th-century **sacristy**, and it is here that we find the most famous painting in all of Verona—Pisanello's spectacular fresco of *St. George and the Princess* (c. 1436), once affixed over the arch of the Pellegrini Chapel, now detached. The left half depicting the episode of the slaying of the dragon is only partially legible, while the right half, in fine condition, describes the romantic scene of the rescue of the princess and the Christian hero's departure for his perilous mission. Pisanello demonstrates a full awareness of the laws of perspective (the foreshortening of the horse is handled particularly well), yet at the same time indulges his taste for a multiplicity of detail and fantastic vignettes. The exotic knights, the steeds decked in gold, the long and lithe princess, the trembling dogs, the landscape dense with details nostalgically evoke the lost age of chivalry.

FROM SANT'ANASTASIA TO THE DUOMO (C5). The streets connecting the two principal churches of the city's center offer numerous points of interest, from beautiful Gothic and Renaissance palaces to glimpses of the "hidden" Verona, only partially damaged during the world wars. Of particular note are two exceptionally dynamic cultural institutions.

On Via Massalongo, a few steps from the church of Sant'Anastasia, is the **Palazzo Forti**, a historic landmark that now hosts the **Galleria d'Arte Moderna**. A sober late-18th-century architecture characterizes the facade and anterior part of the palazzo; the courtyard, the rear and certain interior spaces are instead recognizable as the 13th-century residence of Ezzelino da Romano. Still in the process of working out the definitive installation of the permanent collections (particularly rich in 19th-century painting), Palazzo Forti annually hosts some of Europe's most important exhibitions of contemporary art.

On nearby Via San Mamaso, which crosses Via Garibaldi, we find the late-Gothic **Palazzo Miniscalchi-Erizzo**, presently home to an artistic foundation and an exclusive private museum of Renaissance and Baroque painting and decorative arts.

Palazzo Forti

DUOMO (B5). The cathedral of Verona, dedicated to Santa Maria Matricolare and consecrated in 1187, is an imposing structure, predominantly Romanesque on the exterior and late-Gothic within, set into an articulate architectural complex with elements from the 9th to the 16th centuries.

The facade, the upper part of which was completed in the late 16th century, bears ample traces of the original Romanesque design amongst the Gothic details added later. The variety of its materials creates a lively chromatic dynamism. The double porch over the main portal, erected by Master Nicolò in 1139, constitutes a splendid chapter in the history of Romanesque sculpture, with a rich series of reliefs decorating its elegant structure. Above another carved portal on the cathedral's right flank rises the tall and slightly frigid bell tower, built by Sanmicheli upon a Romanesque base and finished in 1926.

The Gothic aspect of the interior is really the result of work

Liberale da Verona,
Adoration of the Magi,
Duomo.

Duomo, central nave.

Opposite page
Duomo, facade.

done during the 15th century: tall and simple pilasters support vast Gothic arches and cross-vaults. Particularly interesting is the work done by the painter and architect Giovan Maria Falconetto, who in the opening years of the 16th century unified the first two aisle chapels by framing them within a system of illusionistically painted architecture. The central nave resolves in a solemn semicircular ring of columns built by Sanmicheli (1534). The classicizing choir screen serves as an iconostasis for the presbytery, decorated with frescoes by Francesco Torbido based on cartoons by Giulio Romano. Other important works of Renaissance painting can be found in the side chapels, the most notable being Titian's altarpiece of the *Assumption* in the first chapel on the left. Next to it is the *Tomb of Bishop Nichesola* by Jacopo Sansovino. Also noteworthy is the *Mazzanti Chapel* in the right transept.

From the left aisle of the Duomo or from the narrow alley that runs along the exterior, we arrive at an architectural complex of great interest, assembled in large part from remains of buildings from the 9th–12th centuries, though traces from later periods are apparent. An atrium built upon ancient columns conducts into the **Baptistry of San Giovanni in Fonte**, a 12th-century building that incorporates earlier elements (the capitals). In the center is a massive octagonal baptismal font that goes back to the beginning of the 13th century, deco-

Baptistry of San Giovanni in Fonte, octagonal baptismal font with scenes from the infancy of Christ.

rated with marvelous reliefs depicting the infancy of Christ. From here we pass through entrance of the little church of **Sant'Elena**, recast in the Romanesque style on the basis of surviving parts of the original structure, still visible. The exterior portico is from the 15th century. Next is the cathedral's beautiful **cloister**, with its Romanesque colonnade (1140), one side of which was destroyed in the bombardments. The double arcade defining the eastern flank is spectacular. Inside the cloister are the rooms which house the great **Biblioteca Capitolare**, an ancient library founded in the 5th century and later developed, in the 9th century, into a school of calligraphy and manuscript illumination. Conserved here are codexes of historical and artistic importance, as well as the collections of the Museo Capitolare. Our tour of the monuments incorporated into the Duomo concludes with the enchanting **Piazza Vescovado**, one of the more serene corners of the city. The piazza is dominated by the semicircular apse of the cathedral and its stately Romanesque architecture ornamented with an elegant bas-relief frieze. Adjacent to it is the **Vescovado**, a small Renaissance palace with a crenellated facade and a beautiful portal framed by statues. The courtyard is a highly original space, facing out onto various structures from different epochs, including the apses of San Giovanni in Fonte, a stout Romanesque tower and two late-Gothic wings.

Duomo, apse.

Palazzo del Vescovado, portal.

The First Expansion: From Castelvecchio to the Arena

As early as the 3rd century the emperor Gallienus felt the necessity of enlarging the circle of walls around the Roman city that would encompass even the enormous Arena and which would above all resist attack from the barbarian hordes. Larger still was the gigantic series of medieval fortifications (built by the della Scala and the Visconti) designed to close off the center of town as a promontory protected by the curve of the river and blockaded by massive ramparts guarded by castles strategically located in the city and the outlying hills.

It is within this area that our second itinerary unfolds, in effect running from the Adige to... well, the Adige, following in part the line of the 14th-century city walls. Although the distances are slightly greater in comparison to those of the first itinerary, it is advisable to travel on foot, especially between Castelvecchio and the Arena.

There is no better place to begin than the **Castelvecchio**, solid and monumental fortress of the della Scala which incorporates as well a fortified bridge over the Adige. Within the castle is the great **Museo Civico di Castelvecchio**, a collection of Veronese painting and sculpture of the highest order, presented in the context of Carlo Scarpa's unsurpassable installation. An attentive visit requires at least a couple of hours.

Leaving the Castelvecchio, we immediately come upon **Corso Cavour**. A veritable anthology of the history and architecture of the city, its row of aristocratic palaces is bounded at each end by ancient Roman monuments (the **Arco dei Gavi** at the beginning, **Porta Borsari** at the end), while two recessed squares along the street host the Romanesque churches of **San Lorenzo** and the **Santi Apostoli**. The rich facade of the Palazzo Bevilacqua, Michele Sanmicheli's masterpiece, merits particular attention. The Corso ends by folding into Via Oberdan on the right, which in turn opens out onto the "Liston," the broad walkway that defines the left side of **Piazza Bra**, one of the pivotal points of Verona's life and layout, dominated at its center by the unmistakable volume of the **Arena**. The massive stone ellipse draws the visitor on a circular path through the piazza, offering views of important monuments along the way. Following the ring of "palazzi," we come upon a 14th-century double portal flanked by a sturdy tower. To the right is the entrance to the **Museo Lapidario Maffeiano**, a collection of epigraphy and archeological material established in the 18th century by the scholar Scipione Maffei. On the opposite side, atop the 3rd-century walls, rises the **Gran Guardia**. An admittedly circuitous detour along Via degli Alpini, Via Pallone and Via del Pontiere brings us to the **Tomb of Juliet**, a romantic destination in itself, further rewarded by the significant collection of detached frescoes dedicated to Giovan Battista Cavalcaselle. Leaving Piazza Bra by passing behind the Palazzo Municipale, we arrive at the Stradone ("big street") Maffei, which later becomes Stradone San Fermo. This route takes us to the unique basilica of **San Fermo Maggiore**, a Romanesque and Gothic complex whose spectacular apsidal area overlooks the Adige. Its rich and prestigious painting and sculpture collection completes the overview of Veronese art outlined in the Museo di Castelvecchio.

Opposite page
Arco dei Gavi.

CASTELVECCHIO (D3). Majestically overlooking the river Adige from its seven crenellated towers, the castle of the della Scala family was built as both fortress and residence by Cangrande II in 1354–57 on the pre-existing fortifications of the city. A 13th-century stretch of wall divides the building in two parts: to the right is the rectangular main court (military grounds); to the left, the family palace, protected by a narrower double-walled court. Rising from the center is the main tower, or donjon, completed in 1375. The tower marks the point from which the fortified and crenellated **Ponte Scaligero** springs forth to span the Adige with its three arches, presently restricted to pedestrian traffic. The bridge is an extension of the Castelvecchio complex, integrated into its logistical and defensive plan, and constitutes an exceptional example of 14th-century military engineering. In 1945 the bridge was destroyed by the Germans, and then rebuilt in 1950–51 with the original brick and stone retrieved from the river.

Following the della Scala family's fall from power, the castle drifted ever further from its original function as a palace: a munitions warehouse under the Venetian Republic, it was then radically transformed in the Napoleonic era, and used as a barracks during the Austro-Hungarian reign. In 1923 the monument was subjected to an extreme restoration, its former military character being almost completely erased by way of the addition of late-Gothic architectural elements to

The Ponte Scaligero and Castelvecchio.

Castelvecchio, the city-side facade.

Castelvecchio, entrance court.

Castelvecchio, internal facade of the main building, with Venetian-Gothic windows and portico.

the internal facades (taken from Veronese "palazzi" damaged by the high waters of the Adige in 1882), by the repair of the crenellations, and the roofing over of the towers. The castle then became the site of the **Museo Civico**, which from the start has sought to recreate the historical and stylistic homogeneity of the periods represented by integrating painting, sculpture and examples of the applied arts. In 1943, during the period of the Salò Republic, the Castelvecchio was the stage for the "Verona Trial," in which the anti-Fascist leaders responsible for deposing Mussolini were sentenced to death by firing squad. Badly damaged by bombs and isolated by the fallen Scaligero Bridge, the castle remained empty for more than a decade.

In 1957, an extraordinary restoration and museum installation was begun by the architect Carlo Scarpa and the museum's director Licisco Magagnato, and brought to completion in 1964 with the opening of all the rooms. The touch of Carlo Scarpa is already apparent in the entrance court, characterized by statuary, fountains and pools linked by broad courses of stone. To the right are the temporary exhibition spaces; on the left stretches the ancient wall that separates the two courtyards. The facade of the main building is relieved by a Venetian-Gothic portico and windows, between which runs a loggia composed of six arches. Next to the main tower is the most spectacular feature of the museum, the 14th-century equestrian *statue of Cangrande della Scala*, sustained by an unusual projecting support.

Museo di Castelvecchio, medieval Veronese sculpture hall.

MUSEO DI CASTELVECCHIO (D3). The museum's comprehensive collection of Veronese art is distributed through twenty-nine rooms and various levels, including the main tower and the della Scala residence.

The works are presented in chronological sequence, starting with Paleo-Christian objects and ending with 18th-century painting. The first five rooms are given over almost entirely to sculpture (along with some precious examples of *Longobard goldsmithery*), unfolding like a rich statuary parade in close dialogue with the exhibition spaces. Featured in the first gallery is the Romanesque *Sarcophagus of Sts. Sergio and Bacchus* (1179), decorated in vigorous bas-relief. The next three rooms are dedicated to the lively period of *14th-century Veronese sculpture*, with an impressive series of large statues carved from the soft local volcanic stone. While the painting of the same period strove toward courtly refinement, Veronese statuary is distinguished by a strong "popular" accent and by imagery of exceptional formal energy and emotive force. Though we do not know the names of the sculptors, a significant group of stylistically homogeneous works can be linked to the Master of St. Anastasia. Especially noteworthy are the figure of *St. Cecilia* (which Scarpa installed with its back to the viewer to bring out the long braids), the *Crucifixion* in which the characters seem disfigured by their pain, and the no less dramatic *Mater Dolorosa*. The last room on the ground floor hosts *15th-century sculpture*, in which expressive tension gives way to uninhibited linearism.

The Napoleonic wing culminates in the ancient **Morbio Portal**, set into the old walls and restored by Scarpa to function as a central hub of the museum's visitor traffic. One passes from here into the main tower and arrives at the part of the collection housed in the **palace residence**. Both floors are defined by a long salon with windows facing the Adige (where the larger works are displayed) and smaller peripheral rooms. The heart of the collection is its 14th- and 15th-century painting, though there is no lack of sculpture and goldsmithery, including jewels recovered from the Via Trezza and objects from the tomb of Cangrande della Scala. Fragments of the original fresco decorations are preserved on some of the walls. The visitor's journey begins in the smaller rooms, with Veronese painting of the 14th century (panels by Tommaso da Modena and the circle of Turone and Altichiero); the key work here is the *Holy Trinity* polyptych, signed and dated by Turone in 1360. In the last of these rooms, ample tracts of surviving wall decoration provide the setting for a group of panels of exceptional importance, insofar as they are fundamental to our understanding of the transition from late-Gothic painting to that of the Venetian Renaissance. At the center is the enchanting *Madonna of the Rose Garden*, a dreamlike composition in which the Virgin and St. Catherine, accompanied by angels, are seated in a heavenly *hortus conclusus* surrounded by an espalier of roses. Executed around 1425, the painting is generally thought to be the work of Stefano da Zevio, though it has recently been attributed to Michelino da Besozzo. From the same period is the *Madonna of the Quail*, a youthful work by Pisanello, notable for the intensity of its linear elegance: again, the Virgin is placed within a celestial garden distinguished by an acute attention to naturalistic detail. Jacopo Bellini's rare and remarkable *The Penitent St. Jerome* of c. 1436 casts the saint among numerous animals, rocks and other natural elements with an incisive graphic sensitivity and a new, more expansive vision of the landscape.

Pisanello, Madonna of the Quail. Museo di Castelvecchio.

In the main salon are several works of sculpture and the large-scale 15th-century paintings, including the *Eagle polyptych* by Giovanni Badile, head of a family of Veronese artists, and two works on canvas (rarely used as a painting surface before the 16th century): the archaic *Death of the Virgin* by Michele Giambono and the majestic *Crucifixion* by Jacopo Bellini. The last gallery has a fine group of Dutch and Flemish paintings of the 16th and 17th centuries, among which is a *Portrait of a Woman* painted by Rubens during his stay in Mantua.

Ascending to the next floor and entering through the small rooms flanking the salon, one finds selected examples of late-15th-century Venetian painting. The theme of the Madonna and Child prevails, and is exemplified in a particularly sensitive interpretation by Giovanni Bellini (two versions of the work are on display, one entirely by the master and the other executed in part by assistants). Equally suggestive are the treatments of the theme by Francesco Bonsignori, Pier Maria Pennacchi and Nicolò Giolfino. Bartolomeo Montagna's *Two Saints* appear robustly human, especially when compared with Vittore Carpaccio's lithe and graceful *St. Catherine and St. Veneranda*, or to Jacopo de' Barbari's rare half-length of *Christ the Redeemer*. Among the works by Veronese painters, those of Francesco Morone stand out by virtue

Jacopo Bellini, The Penitent St. Jerome. Museo di Castelvecchio.

of their plasticity, while Liberale da Verona indulges in a taste for descriptive detail. The main salon hosts paintings of the early 16th century, many of them tending toward profane subject matter: Giovan Maria Falconetto's *Augustus and the Sybil* is unusual in its profusion of architectural whimsy.

The visitor then enters the Sala della Torre, which contains several important mid-15th-century paintings from the humanist center of Padua. Outstanding among them is the solemn *Holy Family with Female Saint* by Andrea Mantegna, pervaded by a subtle melancholy which renders the heroic canon of the figures poetically human. The *Madonna of the Passion*, a youthful work of Carlo Crivelli, creates an entirely different tone by crowding the space with intriguing minutiae. Francesco Benaglio's *Madonna of the Fan* is a comprehensive essay on the influence of Squarcione on Veronese painting.

Leaving the palace, one passes beneath the main tower through the collection of antique arms, installed beneath the noble gaze of the *Portrait of Pase Guarienti in Armor* (author unknown). Before returning to the entrance building one discovers, projecting from the catwalk, the fascinating *equestrian statue of Cangrande I della Scala* (c. 1335), unforgettable masterpiece of 14th-century sculpture and symbol of the reign of the della Scala family. Seated astride an agile horse, saddle-cloth fluttering, Cangrande seems caught in mid-salute, flashing his famous smile.

The upper floor of the Napoleonic wing is entirely dedicated to painting, predominantly of the Verona school, from the 16th to the 18th centuries. The collection begins with works by Paolo Morando, called "Cavazzola," painter of vigorous and grandiose compositions which reveal his gift for penetrating

Giovanni Bellini, Madonna and Child. Museo di Castelvecchio.

Andrea Mantegna, Holy Family with Female Saint. Museo di Castelvecchio.

Carlo Crivelli, Madonna of the Passion. Museo di Castelvecchio.

Opposite page
Jacopo Bellini, Crucifixion. Museo di Castelvecchio.

portraiture. Along with his works are displayed several small canvases, such as the curious *Young Man with a Drawing of a Puppet* by Francesco Caroto. The next room features two altarpieces by Gerolamo dai Libri, one of which is the popular *Presepe dei conigli* (or "Nativity with Rabbits"). The piercing gaze of the *Portrait of Fra Gerolamo Savonarola*, painted by Moretto, is ever so slightly softened by the proximity of the exotic *Salome* by Callisto Piazza of Lodi.

The third gallery is the most important of this section: in addition to works of the highest order (such as *The Contest of the Muses and the Pierides* by Tintoretto and the *Lady's Concert* by Giovan Battista Zelotti), one finds here the paintings of Paolo Caliari, called "il Veronese." The *Bevilacqua-Lazise Altarpiece* (1548) is essential for understanding the painter's early development and his first independent activity in Verona after having left the studio of Antonio Badile. Crystalline color and powerful compositional energy characterize the great *Deposition*, while the tiny panels comprising *The Story of Esther* are authentic jewels of the art of painting. The remaining rooms document the passage from Mannerism to the Baroque in Verona with works by Paolo Farinati, Felice Brusasorci, Pasquale Ottino, Marcantonio Bassetti, Alessandro Turchi and Pietro Ricchi, and with contemporary works by Palma il Giovane, Claudio Ridolfi and Bernardo Strozzi. Of considerable interest is the collection of paintings done on "touchstone," glossy black panels which create extraordinary nocturnal effects. Two mythological canvases by Luca Giordano open the last gallery of 18th-century Venetian painting, well represented by the works of Sebastiano Ricci, Giovan Battista Tiepolo, Pietro Longhi and Francesco Guardi.

Paolo Veronese, Madonna Enthroned with Saints and Donors (Bevilacqua-Lazise Altarpiece). Museo di Castelvecchio.

Opposite page
Equestrian statue of Cangrande della Scala; installation by Carlo Scarpa. Museo di Castelvecchio.

ARCO DEI GAVI (D4). To the right of the Castelvecchio at the terminus of Corso Cavour, in a garden facing the Adige and traversed in part crossed by a stretch of Roman road stands this elegant monument of the 1st century A.D., built by the architect Vitruvius for the patrician Gavi family. Totally dismantled during the occupation of Napoleon, it was reconstructed in 1933 with the original components. The structure is composed of a single bearing arch flanked by Corinthian columns and crowned by a triangular tympanum.

CORSO CAVOUR (D4). With the Arco dei Gavi at one end and the scenic Porta Borsari at the other, Corso Cavour is the Verona's most affluent and monumental thoroughfare. Lined on both sides by an almost uninterrupted series of noble palazzi, the prevalent architectural taste is classical; the predominant epoch, late-Renaissance.

Starting from the Arco dei Gavi, we first encounter the grand **Palazzo Canossa** on the left, recognizable for its 18th-century balcony decorated with statuary. The facade is by Sanmicheli (1530–37); the interior was unfortunately destroyed by bombs, resulting in the additional near-total loss of Giovan Battista Tiepolo's great fresco (*The Glory of Hercules*, 1760) in the Hall of Honor. Further ahead on the same side, a small courtyard introduced by a Gothic arch opens onto the flank of

San Lorenzo, right side.

San Lorenzo, central nave.

the church of **San Lorenzo**, a diminutive but highly interesting Romanesque building from the early 12th century. The unusual facade is squeezed between two cylindrical towers, the stairs of which lead to the "matronei," or "ladies' gallery." The interior has a central nave and lateral aisles, with the wall surfaces characterized by alternating bands of red brick and yellow ochre stone, typical of Verona's most ancient religious architecture. The matroneo forms an elegantly attenuated loggia supported by columns that run the entire length of the nave, including the transepts and narthex.

Across from the entrance to San Lorenzo is the **Palazzo Bevilacqua** (1530), Michele Sanmicheli's masterpiece of Renaissance civic architecture. Imaginatively and tastefully recombining a variety of architectural motifs from the nearby Porta Borsari, Sanmicheli set the palace on a solid, rusticated ground floor which serves as a base for the balconied loggia of the piano nobile, enlivened by columns carved with spiral fluting and ornamental statuary. Further on is a small piazza that looks onto the flank and bell tower of the **Pieve** (or "parish church") **dei Santi Apostoli**, erected in the late 12th century but renovated many times since, such that only the cloister and parts of the exterior are original. The sacristy provides access to the *Chapel of Sts. Tosca and Teuteria*, a Paleochristian structure reworked in the Romanesque period. Worthy of note is the ceiling, which combines a cupola with a barrel vault. Conserved here is the font traditionally believed to be that in which Matilde di Canossa was baptized. Exiting the chapel and to the right, beneath the shadow of the Porta Borsari, is Via Oberdan, which takes us directly to the Arena.

Michele Sanmicheli, Palazzo Bevilacqua.

ARENA (D4). The third largest of surviving Roman amphitheaters, the Arena has become a major symbol of Verona. Built in the 1st century, later to be enclosed within Gallienus' new city walls around 260 A.D. (the remains of which can be seen in the little piazza behind the monument), it was originally surrounded by a triple-tiered arcade. Rocked by an earthquake in 1183, there remains but a fragment of the Arena's exterior, a mere four bays in length, known today as the "ala," or wing. The internal structure is instead perfectly intact, an unbroken sequence of seventy-two double-tiered arches that form an ellipse measuring 110 by 140 meters. Its grandiosity is further underscored by the interior with its forty four rows of seats and seventy-four gates corresponding to the access stairways. The spectator seating area has been restored and every year the Arena stages a spectacular opera season. This tradition, begun in 1913, is one of Verona's cultural glories: the enormous stage space and the possibility of accommodating some 22,000 spectators (in Roman times it would have held 25,000) consent to opera productions of extraordinary scale and immense power.

Arena, with a view of the "ala," or wing.

PIAZZA BRA (D4). The Arena sits in the center of a vast open square, vaguely triangular in form, largely planted with gardens and surrounded by monumental buildings. The name most likely derives from the presence in the piazza of an uncultivated field, or "braida," also found in the name of a church on the left bank of the Adige, San Giorgio in Braida. The curved periphery nearest the Arena, always full of life, is defined by an uninterrupted row of porticoed palazzi in the clas-

Piazza Bra, the "Liston."

Piazza Bra, Palazzo della Gran Guardia and the Bra gates.

Piazza Bra, Palazzo Municipale.

sical style (16th–18th centuries, among which is the **Palazzo Gustaverza** by Sanmicheli), preceded by the awnings and outdoor tables of numerous bars and restaurants. The broad 18th-century walkway, inlaid with splendid slabs of pink marble, is known as the "Liston."

A grandiose backdrop is provided by the medieval walls and the edifices built into them. At the center are the **Bra gates**, a double arch constructed in 1389 under Gian Galeazzo Visconti, once part of the Cittadella, of which there now remains only a stout pentagonal tower. To the right is a group of 18th-century buildings and porticoes which host the **Teatro Filarmonico** and the **Museo Lapidario Maffeiano**. The latter, a historic institution founded in 1714 by Scipione Maffei, is a prestigious archeological collection of sculpture, tombstones, architectural fragments, epigraphs and steli, displayed in part beneath the portico and otherwise within the recently renovated rooms which, in addition to highlighting individual pieces, help to underline the overall cultural and historical importance of the collection as a whole. Among the more precious works are the Greek funerary steli (5th–4th centuries B.C.), the Etruscan urns, and the numerous Roman reliefs, some of which are of local provenance. Extending along the other side of the Bra gates is the **Gran Guardia**, a hardy palazzo begun in 1610 by Domenico Curtoni, descendant and follower of Sanmicheli. The palace remained unfinished until

1820. The rusticated ground floor is built in part from stones taken from the Arena.

Across the way lies the **Palazzo Municipale**, an ample neoclassical edifice erected by Giuseppe Barbieri in 1838. Its great pronaos and triangular pediment, held aloft by Corinthian columns, is in keeping with the 19th-century taste for ancient Roman temples.

Entrance to the former Capuchin monastery.

TOMB OF JULIET (E5). The last stop on the tour of imaginary sites from Shakespeare's drama of star-crossed young lovers has, despite its meager credibility, a certain evocative fascination. The sarcophagus lies in the crypt of the former Capuchin monastery, of which there remains much, including the cloister and a lovely portico covered by a pergola. The sanctuary has been converted into an auditorium. Also located here is the **Museo degli affreschi staccati** (literally, "museum of detached frescoes"), dedicated to the great 19th-century Verona-born art historian Giovan Battista Cavalcaselle. The collection includes pictorial fragments from the 12th–16th centuries, serving as custodian of the memory of Verona as *urbis picta*—the facades of many of its palazzi were once decorated with frescoes, some of which have been spared from ruin by being transferred here. Among the more significant works are the Romanesque paintings from the votive chapel of Sts. Nazaro and Celso (1180), the Renaissance wall decorations of Francesco Torbido, Domenico Brusascorci and Bernardino India, and above all the reconstruction of the *music room* from Palazzo Guarienti, with its elegant fresco cycle by Paolo Farinati. The little room has been reproduced in its original dimensions, windows and doors and fireplace exactly where they originally were, thus recreating the atmosphere of an aristocratic residence of the 16th century.

BASILICA OF SAN FERMO MAGGIORE (D5). Singular result of diverse phases of construction, this double church is a synthesis of Veronese art and architecture from the 11th to the 15th centuries. San Fermo is, in effect, two buildings superimposed onto one another: the **lower church** was begun by the Benedictines in 1065 on the ruins of the votive chapel containing the relics of Sts. Fermo and Rustico; the **upper church** is instead a glorious creation of the della Scala era, begun in 1313 by the Minorites. The visit starts in the upper church, from which we then descend to the one beneath.

San Fermo Maggiore, facade.

The Gothic facade's single portal lies at the top of a staircase flanked by baldachins formed by suspended arches, and a gallery of pointed arches. The splendid composition of the upper part, opened by four tall and narrow trilobate windows, is ribbed by alternating bands of brick and stone, creating a striking two-tone effect. Along the left side of the church is another beautiful portal, decorated with 14th-century sculpture and a large vestibule. Looking more closely at the exterior wall, one can easily distinguish between the stone of the lower Romanesque church and the brick of the Gothic structure above. This is even more evident in the spectacular **apsidal area**, which overlooks a garden along the Adige. The two

San Fermo Maggiore, the apse end seen from the Ponte Navi.

San Fermo Maggiore, interior of the upper church.

semicircular lateral apses supported by pilasters are clearly Romanesque, while the central apse, built atop a Romanesque base, is a faceted Gothic shaft, crowned by a highly original system of pinnacles and pediments. The whole is rendered yet more evocative by the 13th-century bell tower, and by the lively details of the upper church's exterior.

The single-nave interior is covered by an extraordinary Gothic wooden roof (1314), which follows the profile of the polylobate triumphal arch over the altar. The walls and chapels are profusely decorated to the extent that a first glance may leave the visitor somewhat bewildered. Only after a more contemplative viewing does this palimpsest of ornament begin to make itself legible, gradually revealing the true gems among the plethora of 14th-century frescoes, funerary monuments and Renaissance renovations. Some of the additions from the 16th–17th centuries, if the truth be told, tend to weigh down the graceful Gothic structure, as is the case with the colonnaded enclosure of the presbytery and the huge Baroque *Chapel of the Madonna*, though the latter does host a beautiful altarpiece by Giovanfrancesco Caroto (1528).

Opposite the entrance is an outstanding *14th-century pulpit* in polychrome marble with an elegant wooden pinnacle, framed by the frescoes of Martino da Verona. To the right, a precious fresco fragment of the *Music-making Angels*, an exquisite work by Stefano da Zevio. Among the frescoes on the interior entrance wall, of particular note is the lunette of the *Crucifixion*, attributed to Turone. Turning toward the left wall, we encounter the magnificent *Brenzoni monument* (c. 1426), a masterpiece of late-Gothic painting and sculpture. The sarcophagus, supported by a projection of illusionistic rock, is surrounded by the scene of the *Resurrection of Christ*, an exceptionally animated composition by the Florentine sculptor Nanni di Bartolo. Framing the whole is Pisanello's exquisitely linear *Annunciation* fresco, itself framed by a fine strip of polychrome architecture and crowned by playful Gothic pinnacles and the figures of the archangels Michael and Raphael. From the right transept we descend to what little remains of the **Romanesque cloister** (fragments of sculpture from various epochs), and from here to the lower church, a well-preserved proto-Romanesque structure with a central nave and two lateral aisles defined by numerous pilasters. The *fresco fragments* from the 11th–13th centuries are worthy of note.

From the Medieval Walls to the Renaissance Ramparts

Verona has preserved many tangible memories of its own past as a military stronghold. This longstanding trait, further accentuated in the last century during the Austrian occupation, is embodied in the majestic circle of ramparts that extend along both banks of the river. Our third itinerary unfolds in the sector sheltered by the walls, following the internal circumvallation and using the sequence of city gates as our guiding thread. The few surviving structures from the della Scala epoch in this area are outnumbered by the ingenious 16th-century projects of Michele Sanmichele and the later modifications made by the Austrians.

We start out from **Porta Nuova**, traditional entrance to the city. Nearby is the train station; the broad expanse of Corso di Porta Nuova, lined with numerous hotels, extends northwards to the Bra gates.

Nearby is the Romanesque church of the **Santissima Trinità** which one reaches by way of Via Lanciere and Via Gaspare Bertoni. Following the internal ring-road Alfredo Oriani along the gardened base of the ramparts, we arrive at the Renaissance structure of the **Porta Palio**, terminus of a major thoroughfare of the same name. From here we follow the Vicolo Lungo San Bernardino to arrive at the serene complex of the church and monastery of **San Bernardino**, a fine example of Renaissance architecture and decoration. Continuing along this same street (or returning to the walkway beneath the ramparts), we enter the quarter of San Zeno. The tranquillity of the public squares, the greater openness of the architecture, the noble profiles of the abbey towers prepare the visitor for the splendor of the **Basilica of San Zeno**, a masterpiece of Romanesque architecture and sculpture ensconced in a setting of solitude and silence. The itinerary closes with a walk among the trees that line the raised bank of the Adige (the Rigaste di San Zeno) as far as the small church of **San Zeno in Oratorio**, not far from the Castelvecchio.

Opposite page
San Zeno, portal with external vestibule; rose window by Master Brioloto, called "the wheel of fortune."

View of the 16th-century ramparts.

Porta Nuova.

Corso di Porta Nuova.

PORTA NUOVA AND CORSO DI PORTA NUOVA (F4). The traditional entrance to the city center, the Porta Nuova stands out among the city gates of the Venetian era both for its dimensions and the two round towers on either side. Built by Sanmicheli in 1540, it was heavily reworked in the 19th century during the Austrian occupation. The nearby stretch of 16th-century walls, also extensively modified by the Austrians, is used toward various civic ends: on one side, the **Bastione** (ramparts) **Santissima Trinità** hosts a public park and provides access to the Raggio di Sole ring-road; on the other side, the **Bastioni di Santo Spirito** and **dei Riformati** (best seen from Viale Luciano Del Cero outside the walls) have been turned into gardens which incorporate the city zoo. Additional parts of these massive walls have been adapted for other community and sporting activities. The porta marks the beginning of the wide, tree-lined Corso di Porta Nuova, one of the city's major axes, while the Bra gates mark its end.

Passing beneath the railway tracks and outside of the walls of the city, we arrive at the **Fiera**, or trade fair grounds, which is about a half kilometer from Porta Nuova. Now a major point of reference for the Italian and international agricultural market, the Fiera was established in 1898, specializing at first in the horse trade and then over the years evolving to accommodate multiple aspects of the food, machinery and livestock industries.

CHURCH OF THE SANTISSIMA TRINITÀ (E4). On a secluded side-street not far from the Raggio di Sole ring-road is one of the oldest Romanesque churches in Verona, considered in fact to be a sort of stylistic laboratory for the builders of the Basilica of San Zeno. Founded in 1073 and consecrated in 1117, it was substantially revised in 1130 (of the original building only the northern apse remains), at which time the magnificent **bell tower**, with its quadrangular floorplan and alternating bands of brick and stone, was built. It is not unlikely that this bell tower suggested the form for that of San Zeno. An elegant atrium introduces the Lombardian-style facade, distinguished by its steeply pitched roofline. The single-nave interior houses several 16th-century paintings.

PORTA PALIO (E2). This city gate takes its name from the traditional horse race, or "palio" that was run along the avenue of the same name, starting here and finishing at the Castelvecchio. Its austere classical forms make it the most striking of Sanmicheli's contributions to the military architecture of the city. Begun in 1542, the exterior is defined by three rectangular openings with a metope *frieze* and an elaborate cornice; on the interior, a sequence of five arches framed by engaged Doric columns eases the severity of the rustication.

Michele Sanmicheli, Porta Palio.

CHURCH AND MONASTERY OF SAN BERNARDINO

(D3). This 15th-century religious complex, stylistically on the cusp of the late Gothic and early Renaissance periods, is situated in one of Verona's most peaceful and tranquil corners. Built between 1451 and 1466, it absorbed over the course of the next century such architectural expansions and decorative elaborations as to make it a sort of emblematic gallery of Veronese Renaissance art. The structure as a whole suffered rather serious bomb damage. A serene cloister conducts us toward the simple facade of the church, still possessed of its original Gothic character but for the elegant *portal* with statues, of later Lombardesque taste (1474). The interior has an unusual structure, in that the main nave is flanked on the right by a secondary one, serving to connect a string of private family chapels. Each of them features significant of Veronese paintings of the 15th and 16th centuries (works by Nicolò Giolfino, Francesco Bonsignori, Domenico and Francesco Morone, Francesco Caroto, Antonio Badile). Particularly important is the *Pellegrini Chapel*, the last on the right. An autonomous cylindrical structure designed by Sanmicheli in 1556, it is an excellent example of the measured and imaginative application of elements drawn from the classical lexicon.

San Bernardino, facade and cloister.

*Monastery of San
Bernardino, Sala Morone.*

On the main altar is a large *triptych* by Francesco Benaglio
(1462), evidently influenced by the altarpiece painted three
years earlier by Mantegna for San Zeno. Moving on to the
monastery, one can visit the **Sala Morone**, formerly a library
and still a gorgeous late-15th-century space, with a fresco cycle by Domenico Morone and his son Francesco (1503).

*San Zeno, left side with bell
tower.*

BASILICA OF SAN ZENO (D2). An entire quarter of Verona is given over to the splendidly serene volumes of this outstanding masterpiece of the Romanesque. The urban spaces
surrounding the basilica are characterized by the ancient
monumental presences of various buildings linked to the
church of Verona's patron saint. On the left is the deconsecrated church of **San Procolo** from the 13th century; to the
left of the facade stands a sturdy **tower**, all that remains of the
old Benedictine abbey.

Not far off, Sanmicheli's **Porta San Zeno** provides passage
through the Venetian city walls. Overlooking the whole is the
spare and slender **bell tower**, rising sixty-two meters over
the gardens to the right of the basilica. Begun in 1045 and completed a century later, its surface is defined by the characteristic alternation of tight bands of brick and local volcanic
stone; also typical of the period is the sharply pitched roof surrounded by four pinnacles.

The unmistakable pattern of alternating strips of pale stone
and reddish brick of the Veronese Romanesque marks the
right flank of the basilica as well, accompanied in part by a gallery measured out by small columns.

The present-day church is a sort of compendium of the accu-
mulated heritage of a long series of buildings erected in honor
of St. Zeno. Originally a Paleochristian votive chapel built upon the tomb of the bishop, King Pepin substituted it with a
new structure at the beginning of the 9th century. Devas-
tated by the invasion of the Hungarians in the year 900, the
church remained in a state of partial ruin for the next two centuries until the earthquake of 1117 made a total reconstruction
necessary. The new basilica was built in the very brief period
between 1120 and 1138, thus explaining its stylistic coherence.
Only the lissome Gothic lines of the apse, rebuilt in the 14th
century, belong to another epoch.

San Zeno, facade and bell tower. To the left, the tower of the ancient Benedictine abbey.

The unforgettable facade has taken on a golden tone over time, like a great slab of aged ivory. Its distinctive pitched-roof structure is framed by corner buttresses and articulated by a tight sequence of pilaster strips, accentuated by blind double windows and a cornice of small arch motifs. At center is the great *rose window* known as the "wheel of fortune," executed by Master Brioloto around 1200. The *portal* is introduced by a porch and flanked by wide panels carved with bas-reliefs. The program of these panels as a whole, one of the northern Italy's most interesting Romanesque works of sculpture, is the work of Master Niccolò (c. 1138) and various collaborators. Niccolò signed the hardy and austere *Scenes from the Old Testament* to the right of the portal, while the looser treatment of episodes from the *New Testament* on the left are the work of Master Guglielmo. A third master (who also worked on the portal of the Duomo) is responsible for the *lunette*, which depicts St. Zeno celebrated as the spiritual founder of Verona. Because they are protected by the overhanging porch, these sculptures still bear ample traces of the original painted polychrome surface. Also of great importance are the 12th-century *bronze doors*, composed of forty-eight large square panels with scenes from the Bible and the life of St. Zeno. The astonishing expressive economy and force of the evangelical scenes on the left door, executed prior to the earthquake of 1117, make them especially noteworthy. The functional entrance to the basilica is actually on the left side. Passing by the tower of the destroyed Benedictine abbey (deconsecrated in the late 18th century, the sacred complex was used as warehouse for building materials in the Napoleonic era), we enter the **cloister**, a Romanesque-Gothic structure supported by paired columns and distinguished by a projecting aedicula that serves as a wash-basin. A number of important sculpture and fresco fragments are displayed beneath the galleries, a position which affords an excellent view toward the side of the basilica. From a side portal we enter the luminous interior of the church, a triple-nave structure defined by cruciform pilasters alternating with columns, some of whose capitals are the spoils of war. The presbytery, raised above the crypt, resolves in a tall Gothic choir; the *wooden ceiling* is from the late 14th century. The pilasters,

The Dance of Salome and the Allegory of the Earth and Sea, bronze panels. San Zeno, portal.

Andrea Mantegna, San Zeno Triptych. San Zeno, main altar.

Opposite page
San Zeno in Oratorio, facade.

Stone of St. Zeno. San Zeno in Oratorio. Tradition holds that the first bishop of Verona sat upon this stone to fish in the Adige.

the interior entrance wall and the walls of the nave and presbytery are adorned with a great number of frescoes from the 13th and 14th centuries, some fragmentary and nearly all by unknown authors, which document the evolution of medieval painting in Verona. Especially popular is the enormous *San Cristoforo* fresco on the right wall. Toward the back of the nave a wide staircase descends into the Romanesque *crypt*, with its columns and lovely capitals. A railing protects a recently-built altar in which is preserved the body of St. Zeno. Above the crypt is the presbytery, marked off by an enclosure with statues of Christ and the Apostles (13th century). On the main altar is the great *San Zeno Triptych*, painted by Andrea Mantegna in 1459. A milestone in the history of Italian painting of the humanist tradition, the altarpiece maintains the standard tripartite form while introducing several important innovations, foremost of which is the fact that the three panels, though separate, represent a continuous architectural space executed with a flawless application of the laws of perspective and informed by a sense of classical majesty. The three predella panels are copies of the originals, looted by Napoleon and never returned. In the small frescoed chapel to the left is a polychrome marble statue of the 14th century known as "San Zen che ride," or "The Laughing St. Zeno."

RIGASTE SAN ZENO (D3). To return from the Basilica of San Zeno to the Castelvecchio, one might wish to walk along this tree-lined route on the raised banks of the Adige. Just before the castle is the gracious and secluded church of **San Zeno in Oratorio**, a 13th-century structure with a charming Gothic facade. The church conserves numerous antiquities, among which is the stone upon which, according to tradition, St. Zeno sat while fishing in the Adige.

The Left Bank of the Adige

The geographic traits of the land upon which Verona is built have in large part determined the more intensive development of the right bank of the river. However, evidence points to the likelihood that the first permanent settlement was on the hills of the opposite bank. Ever since Roman times, this area was fortified and included important structures, among which is the still-extant theater. Alas, no trace remains of the temples of the acropolis, though the numerous and beautiful churches disposed along the arc of the riverbank more than compensate for their absence.

For those wishing to follow the entire course of this itinerary, it would be wise to do so by car or public transportation; those who would prefer to stay within the stretch between the Ponte Pietra and the Ponte Nuovo will have no problem travelling on foot. It should be pointed out that the itinerary is contained within the della Scala walls (reinforced later on by the Venetians and the Austrians). One of the main fascinations of this tour lies in the frequent panoramic views of the river, the towers across the way, and the apses of the main churches of the right bank—the view from the esplanade of Castel San Pietro above the Roman theater, for example, is unforgettable.

We part from the **Ponte Garibaldi** (near the Duomo) and faithfully follow along the riverbank, the first part of which is maintained as a garden and characterized by high walled embankments. We soon encounter the church of **San Giorgio in Braida**, announced by its great 16th-century dome by Sanmicheli. A bit further along is the historic church of **Santo Stefano**, with its characteristic Romanesque lantern. Next is the **Ponte Pietra**, which opens onto the archeological site of the **Roman theater**, where one also finds the former Renaissance monastery that presently hosts the **Museo Archeologico**. From the adjacent Piazza Martiri della Libertà, a short detour by way of Via Redentore and Via Borgo Tascherio takes us to the solitary church of **San Giovanni in Valle**. Returning along the street of the same name, we cross the Interrato dell'Acqua Morta, a typical left-bank street. In a nearby piazza rises the robust, though still incomplete facade of **Santa Maria in Organo**. Not far from the church is the **Giardino Giusti**, an enchanting public park. Following in the same direction along Via Muro Padri, we arrive at the great Gothic-Renaissance church of **Santi Nazaro e Celso**.

To get back to the riverbank we retrace our steps briefly and descend along Via Carducci, which bypasses the flank of the Gothic church of **San Tommaso Cantauriense** and takes us to the **Ponte Nuovo**. Continuing along the Sanmicheli river road, we arrive at the **Ponte Navi**, spanning the river toward the scenic red apses of San Fermo Maggiore. The last stop, on the Porta Vittoria river road, is the Renaissance **Palazzo Pompei**, home of the prestigious **Museo di Storia Naturale**.

Opposite page
*The left bank of the Adige,
area of the Museo
Archeologico.*

Paolo Veronese, Martyrdom of St. George. San Giorgio in Braida, main altar.

San Giorgio in Braida, facade.

Michele Sanmicheli, Porta San Giorgio.

CHURCH OF SAN GIORGIO IN BRAIDA (B5). This imposing Renaissance building is dominated by the large and lovely dome designed by Michele Sanmicheli (c. 1530), a principle feature of the skyline of the left bank. The single-nave, barrel-vaulted interior is graced with beautiful 16th-century side chapels. The pictorial decoration is of the highest quality, with canvases and altarpieces from the 16th century. Tintoretto's *Baptism of Christ* on the interior entrance wall deserves particular attention, as do the *organ shutters* painted by Romanino, Gerolamo dai Libri's *Sacra Conversazione* in the fourth chapel on the left, and other works by Moretto, Giovanni and Francesco Caroto, and Paolo Farinati. From the main altar shines the brilliant *Martyrdom of St. George*, the largest and finest work left by Paolo Veronese in his native city. The altarpiece dates from the height of the painter's career, when limpid color and lively light were perfectly integrated into bold and animated multi-figure compositions. Not far from the church, along the first stretch of wall, is Sanmicheli's **Porta San Giorgio** of 1525.

CHURCH OF SANTO STEFANO (B5). Set amidst the houses of a humble residential neighborhood, this ancient church is the fruit of a series of building campaigns from the 6th to the 14th centuries. The exterior is predominantly Romanesque in character—the modest facade, rendered elegant by the usual brick-and-stone pattern, and above all the octagonal lantern with its two levels of double windows, rather close to Lombardian taste. The exterior of the apse is the result of a Gothic renovation.
The shadowy interior carries a powerful emotional charge and offers the opportunity to trace the historical evolution of the building through the 6th (perimeter walls), 8th (columns, capitals, bishop's throne) and 10th centuries (ambulatory, crypt).

Santo Stefano, facade.

The three short naves separated by pilasters conclude with a high presbytery and a raised transept; an evocative ambulatory encircles the choir. Below is the crypt, which repeats the structure of the presbytery above in more condensed form. Also noteworthy is the *Chapel of the Innocenti* at the beginning of the right aisle, built around 1620 and decorated with canvases and frescoes by the finest Veronese painters of the Baroque period.

THE ROMAN THEATER AND ENVIRONS (B5).

The focal point of the left bank of the Adige is the complex of monuments contained within the grounds of the ancient Roman theater, across the river from the scenic apse of Sant'Anastasia. The Adige is spanned here by the **Ponte Pietra**, a faithful post-war reconstruction of the picturesque bridge made up of two Roman arches (toward the left bank), two from the 16th-century (in the center) and one from the della Scala era (at the far right, overlooked by a tower). The diverse phases of construction are distinguishable in terms of both style and the different materials utilized for each.

The **Roman theater**, built in the 1st century A.D., is an imposing assembly of ruins, particularly the vast stepped grandstand, divided into six sections. The whole is rendered picturesque by the presence of buildings from various epochs and by its magnificent natural setting on a hill whose foot is washed by the Adige and whose crest is crowned with cypresses. Particularly elegant are the loggias and terraces above the grandstands. Among the buildings that constitute the archeological area is the little church of **Santi Siro e Libera**, which one reaches by way of a lovely Baroque twin staircase. Only part of the original 10th-century structure is preserved: the graceful Gothic facade is from the 14th-century renovation, while the interior features even later additions, such as the rich

Santo Stefano, left side with lantern.

Roman theater, grandstands. Right, Santi Siro e Libera; above, the former monastery of St. Jerome, now the Museo Archeologico.

choir in inlaid wood from the beginning of the 18th century.
Behind the church, an evocative series of arches, staircases,
columns and Roman ruins leads us to the former **Monastery
of the Jesuits or St. Jerome**, a Renaissance structure which
is today the home of the prestigious **Museo Archeologico**.
Apart from a small group of Attic and Italiot ceramics and a
few Etruscan bronzes, the collections are comprised of art
and objects from the age of Imperial Rome, almost all of local
provenance. Through them it is possible to reconstruct the refined atmosphere of Roman Verona, with its prosperous
trade in *mosaics*, decorative sculpture, and above all *marble
and bronze portraiture*. The monastery's old refectory hosts
the *monumental sculpture* collection; in the cloister are the
tombstones and *funerary inscriptions*; and in the little church
of San Gerolamo (decorated with frescoes by Francesco Caroto, 1508) is the Paleochristian statue of *The Good Shepherd*
(4th century).

Roman armored torso.
Museo Archeologico.

Proceeding from the church we arrive at the terraces, sustained by lovely reticulated walls and providing a panoramic
view of the Adige and the historic center that is truly extraordinary. Other memorable views can be had from the top of the
hill—especially famous are the interconnected esplanades
of **Castel San Pietro** (19th-century Austrian barracks built
upon the ruins of the Visconti castle) and the **Fontana del
Ferro**, or "iron fountain." A few steps away, set among cypresses, olive trees and vineyards, is the small Romanesque
church of **Nazareth**. From Via Fontana di Sopra, we then
head down to San Giovanni in Valle.

CHURCH OF SAN GIOVANNI IN VALLE (B6). A charm-
ing Romanesque edifice, situated in quiet neighborhood. The
church, rebuilt on the remains of earlier structures after the
earthquake of 1117, was consecrated in 1194 and was damaged
in the Second World War. The simple facade is adorned with a
small suspended porch; on the right side, the surviving wings
of the Romanesque cloister lie in the shadow of a massive bell
tower. The three apses are especially well preserved. The triple-nave interior is distinctive in that the central nave is narrower than the side aisles. The **crypt**, which conserves part of
the pre-Romanesque structure, is interesting as well. Two
important 4th-century sarcophagi are to be found here: of
particular note is that of *Santi Simone e Giuda*, decorated
Paleochristian sculptures, though the lid is from the late 14th
century.

San Giovanni in Valle,
facade.

CHURCH OF SANTA MARIA IN ORGANO (C6). Begun in
1481 as the convent church of the Olivetani, its architectural
structure and rich interior make it one of the most elegant examples of the early Renaissance in Verona. It stands in a re-
cess along the Interrato dell'Acqua Morta, typical street of
the left bank that follows the river as far as the Ponte Navi, famous for its panoramic views.
The 15th-century facade is largely covered by a solemn series
of arches, a classicizing touch probably designed by Sanmicheli. From the left side, measured out by graceful little

Opposite page
Ponte Pietra

Castel San Pietro

Santa Maria in Organo, facade attributed to Sanmicheli and bell tower, perhaps designed by Fra Giovanni da Verona.

Santa Maria in Organo, sacristy with intarsia by Fra Giovanni da Verona.

spires, rises the elegant **bell tower**, attributed to Fra Giovanni da Verona, an Olivetan monk who worked extensively in Santa Maria in Organo as a master of marquetry. The triple-nave interior, with its vast choir built for the monks, is enriched by a fine group of *frescoes and altarpieces*, including the festive wall paintings of Francesco Caroto and Nicolò Giolfino in the central nave and numerous canvases and altarpieces from the 16th–18th centuries (Savoldo, Francesco Morone, Paolo Farinati, Guercino, Luca Giordano, Giovan Battista Pittoni). The splendid wood *intarsia* of Fra Giovanni da Verona is one of the masterworks of Renaissance marquetry. Equally spectacular is the *choir* (1491–99), with its carved stalls and backrests inlaid with illusionistic perspectival vistas, trompe-l'oeil liturgical objects and figures of Christ and the saints.

In the center of the choir are two other notable works by Fra Giovanni: the *lectern*, with inlays that simulate open choral books, and the exquisitely carved *candelabrum*. Even more elaborate is the intarsia work that decorates the cabinets in the **sacristy**, again by Fra Giovanni, executed in a later phase (1519). The frescoed lunette of the sacristy, painted by Francesco Morone, bears a portrait of Fra Giovanni among the more illustrious members of the Olivetan order.

Beneath the presbytery is an evocative pre-Romanesque **crypt**, with columns and capitals from the 8th century and a lovely 14th-century relief over the altar.

THE GARDENS OF PALAZZO GIUSTI (C6). Behind the 16th-century Palazzo Giusti, a noble portico leads us into an enchanting 18-century Italianate garden of flowerbeds, statuary, staircases and rocks disposed along the slope of a hill. The architectural organization is especially meticulous in the lower garden, becoming gradually more natural as it ascends the hill. Archeological ruins and a historic labyrinth of hedges underscore the literary significance and the 18th-century taste of the garden. In the upper part, paths and stairways link terraces, grottoes and small architectural structures from which one can enjoy excellent overall views of the park and the city as a whole.

Two views of the garden of the Palazzo Giusti.

CHURCH OF SANTI NAZARO E CELSO (D6). A robust Baroque portal and quiet courtyard introduce the solemn late-Gothic facade of this great 15th-century church, built by the Benedictines on the site of an ancient religious complex. The expansive Renaissance space of the interior hosts a rich collection of 16th-century works of art, among which are the dissembled panels of a *polyptych* by Bartolomeo Montagna, divided between the presbytery and sacristy. Particularly important is the *Chapel of San Biagio* in the left transept. Erected in the 15th century and then decorated by several Veronese artists of the early 16th-century, it houses the *Tomb of St. Biagio and Giuliana* (1508). Especially noteworthy are the frescoes of Bartolomeo Montagna (1504) on the chapel

Santi Nazaro e Celso, facade.

Chapel of San Biagio. Santi Nazaro e Celso.

San Tommaso Canauriense, facade.

walls and those of Falconetto and Girolamo Mocetto (1497–99) in the cupola.

Not far from the church proper is a **votive chapel** dedicated to the same two saints, a Paleochristian structure partly carved from the living rock in which the martyrs are entombed. It is for this chapel that the important 10th-century frescoes, today in the Museo degli affreschi staccati, were originally executed.

CHURCH OF SAN TOMMASO CANTAURIENSE (C5). Standing almost across from the Ponte Nuovo in an area dense with the architecture of Sanmicheli is this great, still unfinished Gothic church, dedicated to St. Thomas Beckett, bishop of Canterbury. Sanmicheli resided in this neighborhood and worked on the interior of the church, specifically in the presbytery, which he remodelled in the Renaissance manner between 1545 and 1550. After the first altar is the great architect's tomb, built in the 19th century by Ugo Zannoni. Also of interest is the beautiful *altarpiece* by Girolamo dai Libri, over the fourth altar on the right, as well as the monumental Baroque *organ*, which has the distinction of having been played, in 1769, by the 13-year-old Mozart.

PALAZZO POMPEI AND THE MUSEO DI STORIA NATURALE (D5). The palace and museum complex lies just a few steps from the Ponte Navi along the Porta Vittoria river road. Among Michele Sanmicheli's masterworks, the palace has a noble and grandiose facade with a rusticated ground floor and a piano nobile defined by arched windows framed by

Fossil of a fish from the Eocene period discovered at Bolca. Palazzo Pompei, Museo di Storia Naturale.

Michele Sanmicheli, Palazzo Pompei, home of the Museo di Storia Naturale.

fluted columns. Equally noteworthy is the porticoed interior courtyard. The palace houses the **Museo di Storia Naturale**, one of the most important science museums in Italy. Recently reinstalled in the interest of didactic clarity, it features zoological, botanical and prehistoric collections. The museum is known above all for its exceptional plant and animal fossils from Bolca, which go back to the Eocene period (30 million years ago) and are in many cases perfectly preserved. Particularly famous are the fish fossils, among which is the large and extremely interesting moonfish specimen. In the vicinity of the Palazzo Pompei one comes upon several important monuments. Following the Porta Vittoria river road, we first encounter a lovely Renaissance cloister, and then, heading toward the Ponte Aleardi, we arrive at the **Cimitero Monumentale**, the Neoclassical central part of which was designed in 1828 by Giuseppe Barbieri, also the architect of the nearby Porta Vittoria, which was built to replace an older gate from the della Scala era.

Returning inside the walls on Via dell'Artigliere, we pass the 18th-century **Palazzo Giuliari**, majestic site of the university's departments of economics, business, languages and education. Further along, on the corner of Via San Paolo, are the 15th-century **Casa Camozzini** and the church of **San Paolo**. Reconstructed in the 18th century and then restored after the war, the church hosts numerous important Renaissance paintings, among which are the *Giuliari Altarpiece* by Girolamo dai Libri, the *Madonna and Child with Sts. Peter and Paul* by Giovan Francesco Caroto, and the magnificent *Marogna Altarpiece* by Paolo Veronese.

Paolo Veronese, Madonna and Child with Saints and Donors (Marogna Altarpiece). San Paolo.

Selected Bibliography

A. Valerini, *Le bellezze di Verona*, Verona 1586.

G. B. Lanceni, *Notizia universale delle pitture di Verona*, Verona 1720.

S. Maffei, *Verona illustrata*, Verona 1732.

A. Carli, *Istoria della città di Verona*, Verona 1796.

E. Sandberg Vavalà, *La pittura veronese dal '300 al primo '400*, Verona 1926.

E. Arslan, *La pittura e la scultura veronese dal secolo VIII al secolo XIII*, Milano 1943.

A. Avena, *Capolavori della pittura veronese*, Verona 1947.

Da Altichiero a Pisanello, exhibition catalogue, edited by L. Magagnato, Verona 1958.

Verona illustrata: il Settecento, texts by S. Maffei, W. Goethe and F. Algarotti, Verona 1959.

L. Magagnato, *Arte e civiltà del Medioevo veronese*, Torino 1962.

P. Gazzola, *La Fondazione Miniscalchi Erizzo*, Verona 1962.

L. Magagnato, *Castelvecchio restaurato*, Verona 1964.

G. Ederle, *La Basilica di San Zeno*, Verona 1965.

E. Barbieri, *Repertorio dei castelli veronesi*, Verona 1967.

G. L. Mellini, *Scultori veronesi del Trecento*, Milano-Venezia 1971.

L. Franzoni, *Verona*, Verona 1978.

Carlo Scarpa a Castelvecchio, exhibition catalogue, edited by L. Magagnato, Milano 1982.

S. Marinelli, *Il Museo di Castelvecchio*, Verona 1983.

R. Chiarelli, *Nuova guida pratica di Verona*, Firenze 1987–88.

Gli Scaligeri, exhibition catalogue, edited by G. M. Varanini, Verona 1988.

Bernardo Bellotto. Verona e le città europee, exhibition catalogue, Milano 1990.

R. Murphy, *Carlo Scarpa & Castelvecchio*, Venezia 1991.

S. Marinelli, *Castelvecchio a Verona*, Milan 1991.

G. L. Mellini, *I maestri dei bronzi di San Zeno*, Verona 1992.

Index of Sites

Photographic Credits
Sergio Anelli, Milan
Archivio Electa, Milan
The drawings were made
by the Studio Margil.

This volume was printed by
Fantonigrafica–Elemond Editori Associati